MW01028603

Every Hour Is Late

EVERY HOUR IS LATE

Poems by

Brian Brodeur

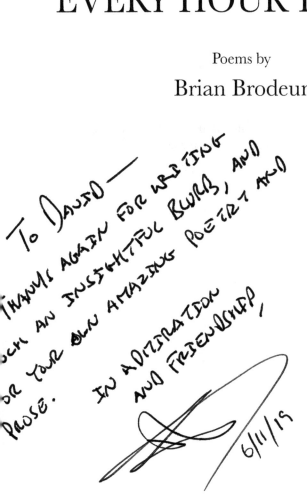

To DAVID—
THANKS AGAIN FOR WRITING
SUCH AN INSIGHTFUL BLURB, AND
FOR YOUR OWN AMAZING POETRY AND
PROSE.   IN ADMIRATION
AND FRIENDSHIP,

6/11/19

Measure Press
Evansville, Indiana

The text of this book is composed in Baskerville.
Composition by R.G.
Manufacturing by Ingram.

Brodeur, Brian
    Every Hour Is Late / by Brian Brodeur — 1st ed.

    ISBN-13: 978-1-939574-30-5
    ISBN-10: 1-939574-30-7
    Library of Congress Control Number: 2018968555

Measure Press
526 S. Lincoln Park Dr.
Evansville, IN 47714
http://www.measurepress.com/measure/

Acknowledgements

The author wishes to thank the editors of the following periodicals and anthologies in which these poems, sometimes in different versions, first appeared:

American Poetry Review: "Talk of the Nation"
Blackbird: An Online Journal of Literature and the Arts: "Deciduous Ode"
Crab Orchard Review: "Blight"
E-Verse Radio: "False Elegy" and "Homeland Security"
Gettysburg Review: "To a Barred Owl Nailed to a Barn Door"
Ghost Fishing: An Eco-Justice Poetry Anthology (University of Georgia Press, 2017): "Cousins"
Hopkins Review: "Expecting" and "Forecast"
Kenyon Review: "Ghazal of the Polar Vortex"
Measure: "Dear Proserpina," "Lake Effect" and "Snare"
Misrepresented People: Poetic Responses to Trump's America (New York Quarterly Books 2017): "Lullaby For an Autocrat," "Landscape with Alternative Facts," "Transcontinental"
Miracle Monocle: "False Elegy"
Missouri Review: "Heritage"
Pleiades: "On Purpose"
Poetry Daily: "A Stand of Swamp Maples in Purcellville, Virginia" (10/21/2013) and "Ghazal of the Polar Vortex" (9/22/2018)
River Styx: "Cousins" and "Suburban Pastoral with Noise Complaints"
Shenandoah: "A Stand of Swamp Maples in Purcellville, Virginia" and "The Picture of Little B.B. in a Prospect of Flowers"
Southern Review: "The Harbor"
Southwest Review: "To-Do List 3.0"
32 Poems: "Lullaby For an Autocrat," "The Register," "Young Achilles at Skyros"
Times Literary Supplement: "To a Barred Owl Nailed to a Barn Door"
Tremble: An Anthology of the University of Canberra Vice-Chancellor's International Poetry Prize 2016 (University of Canberra International Poetry Studies Institute 2016): "Blackout, Imax Theater, Thunderstorm"
Zocalo Public Square: "After Learning of a Friend's Suicide, We Drive to the Cuyahoga Valley National Park"

"Lines Written on the Porch of a Friend's Log Cabin Ten Miles Northwest of Boulder, Montana" won a 2009 Dorothy Sargent Rosenberg Poetry Prize. "Cousins" won third place in the 2012 *River Styx* International Poetry Contest as well as a 2012 Academy of American Poets Prize. "Dead Letters, 1823-4" won a 2014 Academy of American Poets Prize. "Suburban Pastoral with Noise Complaints" won third place in the 2015 *River Styx* International Poetry Contest. "To a Barred Owl Nailed to a Barn Door" won second place in the 2018 *Times Literary Supplement* Mick Imlah Poetry Prize.

The following poems were published in *Local Fauna* (Kent State University Press 2015): "Blight," "Cousins," "Dear Proserpina," "The Harbor," "A Stand of Swamp Maples in Purcellville, Virginia," "The Register," "Returns," "Talk of the Nation," and "Young Achilles at Skyros."

Grateful acknowledgement is made to the following writers, editors, teachers, colleagues, and friends who provided invaluable feedback on these poems and this manuscript: Lisa Ampleman, Eric Bliman, Don Bogen, Michelle Y. Burke, Danielle Cadena Deulen, Katy Didden, James Cummins, John Drury, Claudia Emerson, Daniel Groves, Brian Patrick Heston, Andrew Hudgins, Peter Klappert, Maurice Manning, Sarah Rose Nordgren, Eric Pankey, Michael C. Peterson, Linwood Rumney, Steve Scafidi, J.D. Scrimgeour, Jack Snyder, Kevin Stoy, Chris Tanseer, Christian Terisi, Catherine Wing, and the members of the Portland Accord: Jessica Anthony, Matt Burriesci, Benjamin Chadwick, Paul X. Rutz, and J. Max Stinson. A debt of gratitude is also owed to Indiana University East for two Summer Faculty Fellowships, University of Cincinnati for a George Elliston Fellowship in Poetry, and the Sewanee Writers' Conference for a 2013 Walter E. Dakin Fellowship in Poetry. The author is indebted to the faculty of Indiana University East's English department, particularly Margaret Thomas-Evans, Jean Harper, Laverne Nishihara, Steven Petersheim, and Travis Rountree.

The author also wishes to thank the editors and publishers of Measure Press, particularly Rob Griffith, Paul Bone, and Katie Darby Mullins for the excellent work they do to promote poetry, as well as painter Bo Bartlett for providing the cover image of this book.

Finally, the author thanks his family, without whose love and support these poems would never have been written: Kiley Brodeur, Anna Brodeur, Regina Brodeur, Mark Brodeur, Erin Deslauriers, and Courtney Murphy.

For Kiley and Anna — always
And in loving memory of
Constance Brodeur (1925-2013)

CONTENTS

Vices

Arrivals

Closed in a final rain
Clouds are complete,
Vows of shadowful light
Are vain,
And every hour is late.

— J. V. Cunningham

Ghazal of the Polar Vortex

On my new iPhone, the Weather app defaults to Cupertino —
upper 60s in the Santa Clara Valley. "Cupertino,"

I mutter, hacking snow-crust from the windshield, my khakis
spattered with slush. I dream another life in Cupertino:

In bed with the *Times*, its pages ironed flat by a servant,
I'm propped on my pillow, savoring another cup of tea — no,

a carafe of zinfandel from my own vineyards, eggs Benedict
spewing Béarnaise on a plate embossed with *Cupertino:*

Where Breathing Is More Natural than Death. No crime or poverty.
No churches, voting stations, prisons or libraries — that's Cupertino.

Maybe I *have* been there, or driven through, the light as thick as the oil
in a sperm whale's head, a Cessna skywriting *C-U-P-E-R-T-I-N-O*

above the site where Bautista de Anza's cartographer conjured
the patron saint of mental handicaps, Joseph of Cupertino,

the night they camped along the arroyo they would name after him —
Poor Giuseppe Desa, born in the Italian village of Cupertino

to serve as stable boy to Capuchin friars who thought him simple
until bouts of ecstatic flight lifted him out of Cupertino

and delivered him like a stray balloon to Our Lady of Graces
where he floated over parishioners who swooned, "Cupertino!"

I close Wikipedia, oracle of the digital age, which informs me
autocorrecting with incorrect words is called the Cupertino

Effect: *poïesis* as *poisonous*, *Brodeur* as *saboteur.*
O cathode seraphim, O Holy! Holy! Holy! Cupertino!

Departures

On Purpose

Spring Grove, Indiana, 2016

Our neighbor keeps poisoning raccoons
with peanut butter laced with antifreeze,
    a crumble of crushed acorns
like chocolate sprinkles spooned on soft-serve cones
    he drops in kill traps
or balls-up at the bases of those trees
    they've scaled in vacant properties
behind his house. At night, he scatters scraps.

He says they massacred his hens,
the heritage Rhode Island Reds he'd raised —
    chewed through high-voltage fence
he'd rigged around his yard for home-defense.
    I'm trying not to cringe
at action verbs he spits: "cull," "kill," "erase."
    I nod and offer awkward praise:
He's hunting not for sport but for revenge,

    which seems an older rationale.
He says they breached his walls, like immigrants:
    His "girls," they took them all —
they *have* to die. His thinking's biblical.
    I see the caked smears
of feather-scatter left as evidence.
    Slamming his sledgehammer, he grunts
as he deconstructs the coop he'd kept ten years.

He finger-whistles, shouts, "Come see."
I follow him behind his dirt-floor barn
        to the garbage bins. I wheeze
against the smell of death. Flashing his teeth,
        he lifts one lid to show
a raccoon kit whose underfur looks burned.
        I hold my breath, stare at the ground
and say, "Nice work," before I turn to go.

Talk of the Nation

A student, Naema, calls in from Kalamazoo
and tells the authors of the featured book
that when she studied the triangle trade in school

she imagined a continent populated
by slaves: children literally born in cages
where they waited for their masters to claim them.

In the green light of the dash, my wife snorts —
a sound she makes whenever she hears
a statement so absurd it might be true —

and the esteemed professor emeritus from Hull
admits Naema's right, though only partly,
citing the countless thousands taken captive

by rival tribes ("endemic ethnic warfare"),
how they worked the land of their enemies
and were sold for rifles, rum, calico.

"For *real?*" Naema says. She sounds so young.
Her voice has a raspy aspect as she questions
why Africans would enslave their own people,

but the coauthors explain her misconception:
Africans didn't know they were African
until the Portuguese and Dutch arrived.

"Did *you* know that?" my wife asks, leering.
"Which part?" I say, "The stuff about the Dutch?"
"All of it," she says. "That can't be true."

"Sure it's true," I say, though it's new to me —
the rival tribes, the Dutch, the calico,
the way the Hull professor's tone of stern

authority makes me sneer at my wife's
disbelief instead of conceding my own.
The host of the show thanks his guests, his sponsors,

and, as Naema says, "Excuse me, sir?"
he cuts her off. My wife flips on the headlights.
"You must be right," she says. The theme song plays.

Deciduous Ode

*If any of George Washington's baby-teeth had been kept till
now, they would be put somewhere in a public museum for the
world to wonder at.*

— William James, from a letter to his son,
March 27, 1888

I'd like to think some baby teeth remain,
gnarled
pebbles enameled
with a velvet dust, tumbled, chipped and stained
where they molder in a bin, almost
forgotten mementos
of a former self,
the legendary fruit-tree chopping ghost.
By now, they must resemble chalk
like the Needle Islands off the Isle of Wight.
Displaced, they must emit
the slightest whiff
of sulfuric rot, this set
that shaped the founding phonemes of his talk.

If I found a few of mine, I'd hold them
on my tongue
like cracked aspirin —
not to dull the loss of them, or return them home,
but to hear them strike their still-intact
counterparts, the clack
as they conspire

against me in hushed chitters, sassing back.
        Even their bored successors choose
to stand in a full-pincer flanking position,
                pretending not to listen
                        to each plea and prayer
                I mutter. Still, I feel them loosen
and lean toward the ground. They'll desert me, too.

So why save these, the teeth our daughter lost?
                And why
                in a Ball jar on my desk
        as a paperweight for a to-do list
with half the items left undone, unchecked?
        Because, if I threw them away,
                I'd lose this bone archive
of those years. Because, when I shake the jar,
        they clink like spoons against
                the champagne flutes of wedding guests.
        Because her bicuspids are
                still white as gauze,
        still clenching, knuckle-taut. Because
                it scares me that the first
                to come in weren't the first to leave.

Homeland Security

He stops me on the train. He has a story.
He lost his left arm in Afghanistan
then lost his trailer when the military
quit sending checks, he blames Barack Hussein
who made him place his kids in foster care.
He's diabetic, has PTSD —
he needs his meds, whatever I can spare,
however much my freedom's worth to me.
I say excuse me and try to push past.
He tugs the drawstring of his stopgap belt.
One squinting eye tears up (leaking or crying),
his matted goatee flecks with spit like salt.
I pat my pockets — I don't carry cash.
He grins and says he knows when someone's lying.

Cousins

for David Brodeur (1976-2011)

After the Air Force official
told your folks what happened to you in Kabul,

your brother called. I almost didn't answer.
The bullet to the face, which you survived,

pierced one cheek, he said, then the other,
but you rose from the floor and staggered after

the man who'd shot you, grabbing for his hand
as a second bullet severed your spinal cord.

I was going to say it was too much to hear,
but I didn't have the right — you weren't *my* brother.

He called you a hero, asked if I had any questions.
"Questions?" I said, and he hung up the phone.

It was rare to get the three of us together.
When I flew into DC, we drove to Skyline Drive

in separate cars, and hiked the Whiteoak Trail
to see if the falls were running. They were dry.

On a gravel path, fresh piles of horse dung
swarmed with monarchs and swallowtails

who feasted on something they'd found there.
For a long time we watched their wings

opening and closing in wind, their bodies
pulsing with what resembled pleasure,

their legs and forked tails trembling,
their abdomens thick as pinky fingers.

I don't know why I'm telling this to you.
You were there. You saw the butterflies, the view

of the Shenandoah Valley from the falls.
Draining my water bottle, I coughed and spit —

I promised to join the gym and quit smoking.
Your brother walked ahead. You stayed behind.

We parted at the lot. I can't remember
if we shook hands before we found our cars.

In my rear-view, the sun blazed off your hood,
slices of light flashing as you entered.

Your windshield glinted as if lit from within.
It hurt to look at you is what I mean.

Babble

No Amnesty – Go USA – Go Home
　　　— Handmade sign along US-40,
　　　Preble County, Ohio

The creek we've called *our creek* since I remember
　　　gutters lower now
than I've seen it in years. A new timbre
　　to its voice, as if the slough
it feeds below the gorge's blighted trees
　　　bore more than sediment
through the open throat of the culvert downstream.
　　　Gurgling dissent
　　in runnel-slicks, this spill achieves
its full articulation as rising steam.

The surface stipples, spattering, unclean,
　　　and trickles its litany,
though what it signifies I can't quite glean —
　　its *dos* and *don'ts* spurting tinny
sprinkles that sound more like grievances.
　　　As whorls of algae roil,
commingling with spore-drift, the whole backwash
　　　taints and tints with oil.
　　　Each braided wavelet choruses
in one long sigh, a tinkled prattle-plash.

Or is it spitting praise? An affirmation
　　　of froth and runoff silt,
it dribbles over plates of slatey stone
　　so flood-eroded they chip and split

into the current, the cattails stiff as matches,
       the mud toothed with chert.
Lodged there, a whitetail skull, a spectator
       to this burble and blurt,
    bleaches, watching. Silver twitches
in the creek's descent where stunted walleyes stir.

Fossil Hunting,
Whitewater Gorge

*The other day I was praying over something as I was
running, and I ended up saying to God, "Look, this is all very
well, but isn't it about time you did something, if you're
there?"*
                      — Justin Welby, Archbishop of Canterbury

On limestone terraces,
I sift with my young daughter
for Paleozoic traces:
bivalves the floodwater
exposed within slabs and faces
so brittle she can tear
horn-coral from recesses
with her fingers, without a tear.

She finds a dime-sized shell
she places in my palm,
asking what kind of fossil.
In a gritty, pitted plume,
unfathomable still,
it crumbles, too faint to claim —
though I stammer, squint, and stall —
what it is. So I call it a clam.

What's faith but doubt affirmed
as unconditional,
a clench of old stone formed
when trilobite and snail

sank in a sea now farmed
for feed-corn, mineral
supplanting leaf and frond?
What's love but a denial

of geologic time —
this ruckled bedrock hoard
a cache of heteronyms,
their harmonies unheard?
In a clumsy pantomime,
I kneel to collect each shard —
the flecks all look the same,
the jags on my knees press hard.

As I sort primordial dross,
managing to restore
a few fragments, she's dubious.
I wish, on this inland shore,
that we grow more serious
at our play, the pursuits we share
and those we don't, both of us
more avidly amateur.

Transcontinental

Your safety is important to us, drones
the automated voice. Our seatbelts click
like vertebrae. The cabin dims. *All phones
and portable devices* — it's a shtick,
but I admire the lexicon of flight,
the clarity and lack of condescension
in demonstrations of the brace position
and where to find our life-vests, how they fit.

Cruising in reverse, we leave the gate,
conducted by the flares of semaphores
to idle on the tarmac where we'll get
what we paid for: transference, *metaphor*,
a bag of nuts and room to stow a purse.
As seatmates locate commonalities
in brands of Yoga mats and herbal teas,
I scroll through Twitter feeds. The Airbus purrs.

Our conversations range from Netflix shows
to Trump. A woman laughs: "Why *not* embrace
the lie that saying something makes it so?"
A guy across the aisle says he still prays
before he flies. Another says Facebook Likes
are economic acts and he believes
Eternal Darkness 2 changed his kids' lives.
Beyond our heads the ATCT blinks.

A flight attendant lingers by my leg —
"Your phone, sir, *please*." What if I forget
to power-down? Would the whole fuselage
crush like an empty Coke can, conflagrate?
Preparing for our slog across the night,
the turbine engines hum in unison
the wheezy white-noise whining of their song.
Outside, the stars — trick candles — reignite.

Avocations

To a Barred Owl
Nailed to a Barn Door

In town, church bells rejoice,
        but even the lice
who sheltered in your pinion-down so long
        have been evicted now.
            The slow
bone-sifting wind abrades its brittle song

    on scrub and stubble stalks,
        branches glossed
with ice, the jagged cutlass of your beak.
        Trying not to breathe
            the wreath
of stink surrounding you, I stagger back.

    Is the right response to gaze
        or look away
from the gash in your abdomen, your twisted pose,
        the splay of cartilage
            an image
I can't dislodge, nor the whittled ribs exposed

    where fringe and flesh recede
        in a parody
of the crucifix in a roadside grotto.
        Though I won't reciprocate
            the embrace
your stretched wings invite me to,

I crouch to see whether
fluffs of feather
or dandelion seeds scatter on the berm,
rising to the black glaze
of your eyes
that reflect my small distorted form.

The Picture of Little B.B.
in a Prospect of Flowers

For love of Barry Manilow, his mother
enrolls him in piano after school
with Mrs. Magdalena, who has a tumor
ballooning from her cheekbone like a plum
so bulged with fluid it trembles when she sits
beside him on the bench to rap his knuckles.

One afternoon, she scratches till it bleeds.
Chastising him for his botched bagatelles —
the way he cocks his wrists above the keys
and hums along with Schubert, Liszt, and Brahms —
she smears blood on the Bösendorfer's lid
and slaps the action: *"Pi-ah-nee-see-mo!"*

He stops playing to watch a crimson tear
drip down her jowl and dangle from her chin
before it stains the rug. She yells, "Again,"
and paces, eyes closed as she swats the air
to conduct with one hand, itch with the other.

A month later, Mrs. Magdalena dies.
His mother leads him to the living room
they only use for special company,
the artificial bouquets on the hutch
so dusty he can't tell what kind they are.
She says she's sorry. You *should* be, he thinks,
and asks her if he's finished with piano.
She glares at him and barks, "Go find your slacks."

At the wake, they kneel together by the casket —
the tumor bristling with thick black hairs
slathered with concealer. He can't *not* stare.
His mother rubs his back: "It's fine, you can touch her."
Reaching over Mrs. Magdalena's blouse,
he grazes the tumor with the tip of his finger.
His mother smacks his hand away — "Not *there*."

To-Do List 3.0

Tour Civil War battlefield
in scuba gear. Fell
oldest bristlecone in North
America to find out what it's worth
in rubles, yen, dinar.
Try buying dinner
with antique silk brocade
scored on eBay. Wake with barcode
tattooed on wrist.
Linger over breakfast
of humphead-wrasse
sashimi, arguing which race
to choose for first designer baby. Fib
that test results were negative.
Become unclear
on correct pronunciation of *nuclear*.
Release Asian
carp into sewers. Grease hung
jury with Bieber tickets. Hope
so many bird corpses in Park Slope
will prove a good omen.
Defend congressman's
views on same-sex marriage
as he faces barrage
of reporters' questions
about his daughter who became his son.
Travel gravel
roads blasting Ravel

in search of barns for reclaimed
lumber scam, feel ashamed
as crossbeams scrape sky
like buffalo ribs. Patronize
competing megachurches,
the club called Bottles & Bitches,
the antique mall advertising authentic
memorabilia of Third Reich.
Snap selfie with herd
of pronghorn browsing charred
drought-grass, the butte
shaped like a soldier lacing his boots.

Tritinas: My Father's Vietnam

The less he spoke about what happened there
the more unreal the war became, unchanged.
Lingering on the bottom cellar stair,

he'd stagger close with the same struck-match stare
as if he'd seen someone behind us there —
Did they mean well or ill? Then, something changed.

His conferences of silence were exchanged
for a wasp nest set on fire in vacant air.
Though next year they'd return to rebuild there,

we stared as the nest — there and not there — was changed.

He'd say the past won't hold to one perspective —
a dictum either stolen or invented,
depending on the mood and mask he wore.

Mostly, we wanted answers for the war,
as if it were a question of perspective
which lies proved true and which truths he'd invented.

On days we weren't refused or circumvented,
his jokes and anecdotes depicting war
as boot-camp pranks seemed void of all perspective.

So we invented the war from our perspective.

Left out, the standing mower disappeared
beneath a pall of kudzu. The swing set swelled.
This is why we thought he'd brought the war to us —

to live in its green precincts, dangerous
but beautiful. When coyotes appeared,
he set coil-spring traps by the covered well

and sat in his truck with both hands on the wheel.
As autumn sumac fumed outside the house,
the mist became blown smoke. We disappeared.

Through barred panes, the days welled and peered at us.

Troll

Forget the revolution —
that pair
of Georgia racists
who blasted death-rock from their Silverado
and got ten years for barking threats
at black kids in a bouncy house they shook.
The video
one parent took
went viral. I saved it on my phone.
At the trial, their hands bound with plastic bracelets,
they wept in slatted chairs.

One afternoon in class —
a PowerPoint
about the disparities
among the urban poor, the urban black —
I belly-laughed until I wheezed.
I couldn't breathe. The adjunct asked if I
was back
with them, did I
have anything to add? I asked him was
he aware his Marxist ideologies
were Liberal folklore, sounded almost quaint?

Walking home, a crackling rain
forced me
under a roadside pine.
As drops splashed my eyes (I hate nature),
nothing in that scene seemed mine.
Not the messenger bag I wore. Not my own hands.
Unsure
when it would end,
or *if*, I wanted to run,
but felt stuck to the trunk, set with a pin:
a moth under glass in a frame.

I get it. I grew up poor.
Working-class.
My dad banged nails. My mom
took people's kids away — that's what she called
social work. I couldn't fathom
home-schooling six of them in a modular
in Plainfield,
Indiana, the blare
of IND. I could've left home or
worked shifts at Frito Lay, becoming them.
I chose the first-gen pass.

Thick fog concealed the road —
at least
I could *hear* the cars:
the bacon-fat sizzle and hiss of puddles

exploding in static-swishes, tires
clattering asphalt cracks in the rutted street.
The less
I *tried* to see
the more I saw, though blurred,
of a far gray meta-verse enclosed by bars —
glimpsed only, though, then lost.

After the verdict, the woman
trembled,
pleading without
lifting her chin from her chest, the courtroom packed
with press: "I want you to know that
wasn't me, that is not *me*." Who was it then?
Alt-fact,
her claim, though thin,
intrigues: What does it mean
to argue in one's defense an ad-hoc out-
of-body hack, fumbled?

Intractable as granite,
the world
within this one,
whether far or gray or barred — we're barred from *it*.
Some see the interface, the bones
of its architecture. None see the thing itself:
the meat
on the freezer shelf

that doesn't reek or rot,
Pythagorean cycles — zeros, ones —
purged of any word.

I'm not racist, I'm *not*.
My professors
scoff, so I say what
they expect — maybe even what they want
me to say, though they'd never admit it.
Do they think they don't lie? Why not shout, "Read
Mencken!" or taunt
them with Paul Gottfried?
Nothing's bought
that isn't sold. Played or played out. Just wait
and see who forfeits and who scores.

Forget the revolution.
It's here,
writhing and alive.
It crouches for the right dystopian
who knows the best prod for the hive
(*alt-right:* the phrase itself might well mean *wrong*)
is spin
that sounds like a song
we've heard before but in
a safer form — the MP3, not live —
until it's all we hear.

Honey Locust, October

Little flames
extinguish
on clay:
a phylum
of decay
no less lush

than a bowl
of jam plums
left to rot,
the bole
a riot
of legumes

split, their pulp
seeding gutters,
husks crisp
in coiled clumps
that rasp
when gusts

rattle them,
compound leaves
flickering,
vein to stem
clinging —
each one alive

in wind
no defense
opposes,
though the end,
its hushed applause,
makes no sense.

Returns

There is no innocent explanation.
— Bernard Madoff, 2008

Relieved when they arrested me, I slumped
in back of the cruiser with my head

between my knees, and smiled —
I didn't have to lie anymore.

Even being in lockdown was like vacation.
I was free. The inmates all knew me.

"Hey, Bernie," they'd say, "how'd you steal
that money from those old Jewish ladies?"

"Fuck them," I'd say, "I floated them for years —
If anything, *I'm* the victim here."

Why should I be ashamed? My life's over.
Or else it's just begun — either way,

it doesn't change the fact my son is dead.
The day I heard, I was walking the track

when a guard told me I had a visitor.
Through plexiglass, I saw my wife had been crying.

I buttoned up my standard-issue khaki shirt,
sat at the booth that stank of disinfectant

and lifted the receiver to my ear. . . .
It's not what he did, but how he did it.

I picture him driving to Home Depot
for a length of rope. Waiting for the kids

to fall asleep before he wrote his note.
Kicking away the office chair.

He made his choice — I know it's not my fault.
I called him once last year before the trial

to tell my side, how I'd been used,
and how I'd never lie to family.

He didn't speak, but he was listening.
I heard him breathing at the other end.

Forecast

Impossible to comprehend the wind —
its broken dialectic with the firs
crackling like a cracked CB scanner
in the slightest murmuring off Puget Sound,

distinct in logic, rhetoric, and tone
from the hurricane dismantling a pier
on Narragansett Bay, its ragged power
to scatter planks and pilings in the foam.

As Sandy surges, we talk politics
in intervals between raw bursts of thunder,
debating *global warming/climate change*,

the storm door clinging by a rusty hinge,
the air inside the room shifting like air
inside a bell before the clapper strikes.

Hazards

Blight

I was born in a city with a river running beneath it.
Summers, the chemical stink of textile dyes
seeped up from viaducts under the streets.
Two bridges spanned a lake to the northeast
that fed into the river underground.
We heard of those who walked the bridges at night
and climbed guardrails, who scaled trestles
to leap into the water and disappear.
We heard a lot of things: the stillborn boy
dumped in a Papa Gino's ladies' room,
the Service Master van with painted windows
by the playground woods where two teenage girls
were found in a ditch near Great Brook Valley.
Bored, we'd steal cemetery flowers
and pitch them at each other, shattering
blooms with a bat that gave us special power
because we heard Yastrzemski owned it once.
Sticky with strips of black electrical tape,
it belonged to Joe Camuso down the street.
When Joe showed up one day without the bat,
he said his dad had split it beating a man
he'd caught that morning pissing on their stoop.
"Dad wasn't even drunk," Joe said, grinning.
Police tape fluttered there until it tattered.
The night Joe's dad got off on self-defense,
my own father staggered home after the party
at Stoney's Bar, waking my stepmother.
I heard the thud of boots dropped on the floor,

voices murmuring through drywall.
"I'm sick of all these Blacks," he said. She shushed him:
"Quiet, the kids will hear." "Sorry," he said,
"I mean these *African Americans*."

Shelter

A sleet storm heaves in blasts that spit
and rattle the plexiglass
that makes us ask too much of it:
to shield our huddled mass

of commuters jostling for a spot
away from pelts and shrieks
of ice-sheets stinging, tears and snot
freezing to our cheeks.

A privileged few pack into the back
(they reached the shelter first).
They watch the ceiling. Fat drops smack
and whorls of nimbus burst.

Others shiver half-under the eave,
squinting at the sky,
pant-leg, dress-hem, and jacket-sleeve
stuck to their skin. Though I

try to avoid the glares of some
exposed to the wind's chafe,
their faces gleam as I text home
how lucky I am, and safe.

False Elegy

Our neighbor Ted, a blind man, died last month.
We didn't know his name until a friend
asked if we'd heard about the accident:
a rainy day, roadwork, a car's bald tires.
My wife asked why I was so upset —
I never even knew the guy's first name.

"That's *why*," I said, "We should've known his name."
"We just moved in," she said, "It's been nine months."
"Ten," I said, "Why aren't *you* more upset?"
I heard her Skyping later with a friend.
Griping about the roadwork (her new tires),
she predicted it would cause an accident.

I glared at her: "*Another* accident."
When she logged off, she shouted my full name
like my mother would. "Sorry," she said, "I'm tired."
I asked if I should buy a card — or was a month
too long to wait? She nodded, "For a friend
or relative. But buy one. You're upset."

I asked my therapist if he could set
me straight: "Zoloft?" He said the accident
brought back my cousin's death, how I unfriended
his wife who'd photoshopped his rank and name
above a dead bald eagle. "That was months
ago," I whined. "Relax," he said. I tried.

I bought a card (fall leaves, rain) but retired
it to the junk drawer. What if it upset
Ted's wife? My wife told me to wait a month
and I'd forget about the accident.
I waited. I started hearing Ted's name
in conversation. I annoyed my friends.

I couldn't sleep. Why bother to befriend
new people anymore? My thoughts felt tired.
My voice, my attitude, even my name.
My wife was tired, too: "You're *still* upset?"
"Yes, I'm upset, there's been an accident."
"Enough," she said, "You've been this way for months."

The months dragged on, the year. I felt less tired,
upset about my non-friend's accident.
I mailed the card but didn't sign my name.

Active Aggressor

A text-update vibrates my phone:
one suspect, armed, reported on
the quad. *Seek shelter. Lock the door.*
Remain in place. With info or
emergencies call 9-1-1.

I kill the office lights, drop down
under my desk—That's *it?* I'm *done?*
I should've said *I love you* more.
My phone vibrates:

White male, gray t-shirt, jeans, handgun.
A fly floats toward the transom, gone—
I listen to the corridor:
shoes click across the porcelain floor.
I sweat and breathe. Am I alone?
My phone vibrates.

Seascape, Unattributed

My wife snorts at her phone ("This pic's the best"):
    our daughter, at the Dollar Tree,
sporting kitty ears and biting her tail.
I snort, too, and toggle through shots until
    I see a selfie of a woman's breast
        post-surgery:

    a bandage, sweat-blotched, snipped, blood-crusted stitches
        circling the nipple
like caterpillars, areola stretched
so thin it looks smeared on her skin, as if sketched
    with bruised pastels, a hyper-realistic
        bafflement of pixels.

    My wife's mother, home from her oncologist,
        called last night to beam:
She finally felt well enough for mint
ice-cream, her favorite. I asked what she meant —
    "Can you babysit?"
        A joke. What's wrong with me?

    I pass back my wife's phone but forget to fade
        the screen. I start to drift
to the next room. "Oh," she says, as I reach
the kitchen table. I don't want to broach
    the topic I've been struggling to evade.
        This latent grief —

I hear it tremble in her voice each time
      she says, "Mom's fine."
Her face squinches around the words, revealing
those tiny creases like cracks in a ceiling
      you don't notice until, one stalled bedtime,
          you stumble on the rug to feign

      a gunshot to the sternum as your daughter
          aims animal balloons
like AK-47s, "Bang, you're dead!"
Lying on your back, a zombie dad,
      you trace the capillary clefts in plaster
          from wall to wall: age lines.

The chili pot burbles, overfull.
      By the microwave,
a wedding gift from my wife's mother hangs:
froths of spray suspended over crags
      like feathers of some buckshot ocean-fowl,
          cloud-mottled waves.

If *mystery*'s too strong a word, the gift's
      become a source of lore.
My wife and I, up late with too much wine,
have slurred competing speculations why
      the mother-of-the-bride would buy us *this*
          instead of a drink chiller.

My wife's mom left her church when she left home
      and doesn't nag or push
our daughter's baptism, which we've refused.
But since her diagnosis she alludes
      to angels: Why don't we believe in them?
          They're everywhere, watching us.

Each Father's Day, she drives to Galveston
        to visit her dad's grave.
She talks to him and toasts him with a fifth
of Beam, his drink. I envy her her faith.
        Knowing he hears her, she feels better: stoned,
            but less bereaved.

I ask my wife again about *"La Mer"*:
        "Why do we hold onto it?"
Though years ago she stopped shifting it from
the kitchen to the closet to the bathroom,
        she still can't decide. I've always liked it more
            for the frame, not what was in it.

Blackout, Imax Theater, Thunderstorm

As ushers pace the aisles and yell, "Stay calm!"
the guy beside me jokes about the myth
of women and children first from sinking ships.
His Skittles click. His phone glows in his palm.
I count twelve phone-glows in the multiplex —
they clarify the dark, giving it shape
like searchlights seen far off, too far to help.
He knocks my elbow from our shared armrest
and kicks my sneaker, grunting, "My bad, Bro."
I clutch my bendy straw like it's a shiv.
According to the Scale of Kardashev
which ranks humanity at Level Zero
(still groping toward home-planet mastery),
we might reach Level Two in a thousand years
if we can engineer a Dyson Sphere
to sap a star of all its energy.
On Earth, the guy beside me starts to snore
but wakes when thunder shakes the balconies.
He slurps his Diet Pepsi to the lees
and claps between each burst, "Encore! Encore!"

Heroin

for D.R. (1980-2017)

A month after I missed the closed-casket
of a childhood friend, I saw his folks.
　　None of us expected them to make it

to my sister's wedding. The father waved a fork
　　and pointed at the empty chair beside him.
He slapped my back and picked a fleck

　　of parsley from his teeth. I said his son's name,
apologizing, and asked how they were —
　　thrown-off by his casualness, ashamed

for not joining them sooner. Did I want some gruyere?
　　The father talked. The mother drank too much.
She wouldn't stop smiling and stroking my hair,

　　her nails scraped my scalp. I didn't touch
the plate they'd fixed me, glancing around for my wife.
　　I watched a vase of parched hydrangeas slouch.

From the open casement windows I caught a whiff
　　of low-tide stink. The mother asked no one
why they'd built this hall so close to the rotting wharf. . . .

　　When I heard, I remember thinking *heroin* —
I may have even muttered the word out loud
　　to my own father, whose muffled monotone

explained, "It is what it is," like liquid lead
    pouring through the phone, yet measured, dry,
as if he'd practiced it before he called.

    The mother wiped her cheek (grit in her eye)
and sneezed, her knee bumping my knee
    as the father munched kale and sipped his rye.

    I said I should find my table, my family,
but the mother kept squeezing my hand.
    Whether he meant it for his wife or me,

the father said, "Be good." Speckled with sand
    from the centerpiece, her fist unclenched, retracted.
"Just go," the father said, the one who'd found

    his youngest at the studio he rented
tangled (I'd later learn) on a futon
    he'd owned since college. The father sat on the bed

and groaned for his son to wake — the way he'd done
    when his son was late for school — but he saw one arm
dangling over the edge like rain-pocked stone.

    Then, the father knew. He tucked the arm
under the covers and dialed 9-1-1,
    switched off the bedside lamp and left the room.

Snare

*What is a song but a snare with which to capture the
moment?*
— Eric Pankey

Embowered like a heart behind a wall
of ribs and viscera, a cardinal pipes
staccato trills across the lawn, his call
not quite a song: one-note, a censor's bleeps
against the wind's invectives in the trees,
a smoke detector's chirp for batteries.

Whether he trolls for food or territory
or to entice the less conspicuous sex
from hiding in the icy understory,
his snare has had the opposite effect:
above the net of limbs, a red-tail whirls;
a cat's claws rasp against the poplar's burls.

Vices

Book XIII

Fleeing a burning, ravaged city in Asia Minor, a group of displaced exiles set sails in desperate search of a new homeland. Instead of welcome, they encounter distrust and hatred.

— Michael Dirda,
reviewing David Ferry's *Aeneid*, 2017

All I remember now are portages:
a book left in the rain that fused its pages
and blurred what text remained unreadable.

Still, I can taste the meat of a slaughtered bull
in a city some said wronged us in some way,
though I can't think if anyone knew why.

To note the *here* in *there* once seemed enough:
the crow-gleam of charred trees where a fire was snuffed,
the moon, the brightest bead on unseen thread,

and the sky, our abacus. Heard or unheard,
the melodies of home resounded nights
that seemed to drown (I *saw* them) in our nets.

The plot is not the point. Our destination
looked much the same as where we first put in.

Landscape
with Alternative Facts

An invasive species doesn't have to be from another country.
— National Wildlife Federation.org

I was never born.
  I subsist
on rain and iron
  deposits
lodged in public land
  as I bore
through the ground, blind.
  Like amber,
I confine caught life:
  a canker within
an Eocene leaf.
  Whittled thin,
I needle
  toward the surface,
earth-addled,
  the blade of my face
beginning to crown
  through gravel
I claim as my own —
  the stripped vale,
the fractured
  asphalt,
the last word.
  Who could fault
the house fire
  that warms the night?

The noose for
  the dead man, his note?
I know I exist
  because I
obstruct all exits.
  I deny
the dust, resist
  like a swollen tick.
All the rest
  is myth, politics.

Young Achilles at Skyros

Bored of playing swords, barefaced Achilles
combs the shoreline for washed-up debris.
From behind the rotting hull of a vessel beached,
he watches a man work a spit into a mackerel
and wipe gore from his knife on the rags he wears —
Why should *he* get to light fires on the sand
and swim in the ocean without a chaperone?
Achilles lobs a stone, splashing a tide pool
beside the man whose feet spatter with foam.
"I want you off my beach," Achilles screams.
"*Your* beach?" says the man. "That's right, my beach."
Achilles hurls one bigger than his fist.
"Yes!" he hisses. The man's brow bleeds —
he clasps his hands, asking for mercy, mercy.
Achilles smiles: Why *shouldn't* he be feared?
He wishes he could throw stones at the sea
and stop the senseless tide from always shifting.
The man has stopped moving. Achilles waits
until he's sure, then walks toward the body.
Up close, the man looks young. His skinny arms
could be a boy's arms twisted beneath him.
Sand fleas flick in and out of his mouth.
Careful not to step in darkened mud,
tender-heeled Achilles bows to stroke
the man's wet face and hair, closing the eyes.
"There, there," he says, "that's better, go to sleep."

Lullaby for an Autocrat

One by one, in every booth, the naphtha jets were turned down
and the canvases pulled over the little gaming tables.
— Dylan Thomas, "After the Fair"

Who but an after-hours guest
would notice, snagged in grass, the flit
of popped balloons displayed like flags
of fallen cities: Babylon
and Ugarit? Who'd pat the head

of a dozing lion, underfed,
and clap away the haloing
of gnats above its jangling tags?
Who'd prowl beneath the brown bat's flight
to peep the bearded lady's breasts?

Relax. The fairground tents, beset
by shadows, burst with straw crushed flat
as turnstiles click and moonlight drags.
Be seated now, be still, and lean
on bounce-house walls not yet deflated.

Don't fret what So-and-So has stated,
how awful much you feel alone.
Ignore the mounting garbage bags,
the naphtha jets that immolate
the carousel. You need your rest.

Sleep tight and dream these wooden beasts
run-through with poles stampede the light
that inches toward the oil-soaked rags
you bunch as pillows. Loaf, recline
and hug for warmth your burning bed.

Dear Proserpina

Ain't no sunshine when she's gone.

Maybe you're right. My love for you *is* cruel —
my late-night appetites and gifts that sparkle.
In bed, I'd slip a finger underneath

your nightclothes to see if you were sleeping.
You always were. Except the night you muttered,
"Kill me, please," laughing a throaty wheeze

that startled me. I tried to comfort you.
You rose with a start, blinking, and looked at me
as if you'd never seen my face before.

So often I misjudge these situations.
Through a tangle of candelabras and cloth flowers,
I watch you read a novel across the table.

I say, "I'm happy," and I force a smile.
"Me too," you say, "Now let me finish eating."
And immediately I wish I'd said nothing,

that every utterance could be taken back,
the words spoken in anger, the tender things.
Sometimes your skin against mine feels so real

I don't know what to think, what I *should* feel.
When I touch the fuzz on your belly, you say, "Stop,
quit it — you're tickling," and you turn away.

Last night, I roamed the halls, looking for — what?
I couldn't say, except I thought I heard
a tune I used to know seep through the walls.

Some old chorale, stiff and faintly martial.
I clapped my hands to make the music stop.
It only grew louder — I was overcome

with the desire to dance, to stomp across the floor
and see my face reflected back at me
in polished stone. I romped until I tired.

I swear I smelled your perfume on the air,
the scent of calamus and coriander.
I scanned the chamber. How long had it been

since I'd visited this wing of the ancient house?
It amused me to think you've never seen
these musty rooms: long floral papering

still clinging as it tatters at its seams.

Suburban Pastoral with Noise Complaints

His wife, still half-asleep, groans, "Call again."
He rises to the window, peering through
at kids shucking their clothes off by the pool
to dance around a fire-pit heaped with ashes —
hard bodies flickering in halogen
that makes the water smolder as it splashes
on grass, on boxwood hedge, on sagging porch
like spatter spurting from a welder's torch.

Behind the swings, a girl his daughter's age
squats on a lawn chair. As she thumbs her phone,
her face and throat look pressed in Styrofoam —
her naked breasts, still glazed with wet, glow green.
If he approached her now . . . she'd run away.
His nose against the screen, he smells chlorine
and sees, tattooed in red between her breasts,
a heart in razor-wire — or else, a fist.

Dead Letters, 1823-4

[I]t is all very well if one died at the end of a Tragic scene after playing a desperate part — but if one lives & instead of growing wiser — one remains the same victim of every folly and passion — without the excuse of youth & inexperience — what then?
       — Lady Caroline Lamb, 1824,
            six months after the death of Byron

My Dearest Lord —
             I tell you feelingly
you could not lay me lower than you've done —
declaring without doubt, & publicly,
that you would see me in a "strait-waistcoat"
if I did not refrain from writing you,
that I conceived mean arts to blacken you —
but, on my life, whatever my life means,
I never have deceiv'd or perjur'd you,
& say with countenance as guileless
as an open grave: I would you lov'd me less.

I think I love you with the eyes of Sense
as with the eyes of Passion I once lov'd —
& would as well be batter'd, clapp'd in chains
& dragg'd on wattles through the Palace Yard
than see you not, nor hear from you a word.
Why should my hopes for you be timorous?
I hear you sail for Cephalonia —
I wish you weeks of sun & tranquil seas,
but, as you know, my wishes all have teeth.

My Lord & Master —
                    You have called me cruel —
was I cruel when you first entreated me
to kiss yr lips — &, thinking I'd displease you,
I could not stay my body from your own —
Was I cruel then? — were you? — Are we cruel now
to hide behind the lappets of these lines?
I find, because I can't recall yr face,
that you've become to me a cautery
which burns my retinas, singeing my vision —
You *blind* me, Sir — &, like a fervid child
who has no higher proof of adoration,
I cannot keep from staring at the sun.

The Harbor

Me, me alone, with fetters firmly bound,
The gods allow to hear the dangerous sound.

We rowed all afternoon and didn't speak.
When beeswax in our ears dripped down our beards
we heard the singing: women's voices trilling
a melody we knew but could not place.

We dropped our oars and leaned against the gunwales.
We looked toward the harbor dotted with rocks
where groggy seals barked and sprawled, their figures
frisking in the spray of combers breaking.

The song grew louder then, flooding the air
with strains that made our hearts beat in our ears.
Our pumping blood accompanied the music
it hurt to hear but hurt more *not* to hear.

The seals lifted their heads as if to hold
the song inside their mouths, their jaws gaping.
Sleek bodies bobbing to the steady rhythm,
they swayed together in a kind of trance.

Misenus broke the spell. He dropped the vat
of wax at our feet, pointed, glared at us
until we pressed fresh clumps into our ears.
Our thoughts whirred like wind inside a shell.

Riding a long swell, we rose and fell
into open water, leaving behind the islands.
The surface of the sea glinted like fish scales.
The green blades dipped in waves, and scudded foam.

We wanted to *be* the seals — to feel our bellies
slap against cold stone, our wet fur shining.
We wanted to crack raw mussels with our teeth
and doze beside each other in the sun.

Arrivals

The Register

On the steps of the public library this morning,
a man in waders pressure-washes marble
glazed with a patina of pigeon shit.
Billows of frothy spray spew from his nozzle
as he flicks his wrist to increase the stream
and stares at a girl in spandex shorts
who chains her bike to the rack, unclips her helmet
and shakes out her damp curls.

The man's radio blasts Weekend Edition:
Renée Montagne and Steve Inskeep announcing
that four-hundred years ago this week
Thomas Thorpe entered into the Stationer's Register
his right to print the first of Shakespeare's sonnets.
When listeners were asked what words of love
in our time could last as long, they responded:
the songs of Kris Kristofferson, the rhymes of 50 Cent. . . .

I'd like to enter into the Register
how this man grins at this girl, the way he leans
into the wind to angle the pressure-washer
mizzling daylilies with spits of mist
as she ascends the steps, ignoring him
and the jets he spurts across the façade, bright bands
of yellow and indigo hanging in air
just long enough for a kid to yell, "Rainbow!"

Expecting

We haven't slept together in six weeks —
I'm keeping track. In bed, she says, "Let's try."

I bleat my Yoda voice: "There is no try.
Do, or do not." She groans, strips to her socks.

"I'll brush my teeth," I say.
                              "Do you *have* to talk?"
"Sorry," I say.
                "And don't apologize."

I click the lamp. It feels like exercise
straining for the right angle. My back cracks —
"Like this?" I ask. "Or this?"

                              After, she yawns:
"It's cold in here." I pinch the sheet between
my toes, sliding it up to cover her.

"Am I still beautiful?"
                    "Of course you are,
but I have to pee." I peck her damp forehead.

"Did it feel *different?*" she asks.
                              "Crowded."

A Backward Glance

As he referred to "yesterday," he now gestured, not backward,
but forward. As he explained "tomorrow," he gestured back
over his shoulder, up toward the ridge.
       — Kensy Cooperrider and Rafael Núñez,
       "How We Make Sense of Time"

Vacuum pumps, hobbles, and pasteurizers
still loitered in the corners of the barn,
the stalls emptied of Holsteins, clover and vetch
emitting a ghost-odor from the loft.
    September. Mom and I had driven out
to see the family farm in Leominster
before it sold to Kettle Brook Golf Club.
    Outside, we reached a galvanized-steel gate,
the knot in rope that cinched it shut still holding
where post and gate met, long after the one
who'd tied the knot had left with the final herd
to pass there, and the pasture where they'd grazed
clotted with plants we'd called "prickers" as kids.
    "Gone," she said, as we trudged chicory
and found the backyard where she'd learned to pluck
waterfowl her uncles bagged at Christmas,
dropping the bloody quills and puffs of feather,
her fingers raw from working in the cold.
    The house was locked to us — we'd tried each door.
By the dried-out slurry pit, she swatted behind her
as if against an onslaught of black flies
nipping from the rear, but she was gesturing
to bulldozers and a crane parked at the edge
of the property, the site of fairways to come,

a tavern where her last remaining uncle
would nurse Michelob Lights and watch the rain
shift to sun-glaze lacquering man-made hills
he didn't recognize, hazards and roughs
where he'd dragged calves from heifers in the spring.

    The future was behind us. We'd walked into
the past. From where we stood on a squat rise
studded with lumps of quartz like plaque in teeth,
we could see a burn-pile and a gutted stable,
the heart-shaped tracks a deer had left in mud
meandering through fields and the woods beyond
empurpling with evening coming on.
Construction on the clubhouse had begun
and we could hear a backhoe striking boulders
to gouge the new foundation farther out
from Cortland orchards flanked by Northern Spy
whose trunks were still tar-banded, each gnarled tree
drowning in a flood of honeysuckle.
    Unknown, that place became its leaning house,
maple saplings inching from the gutters
straighter than the house itself could manage,
its batten shutters hindering our view
of a bare interior, a vacancy.
    As we walked to the car, my mother asked
if I would drive — I had my Learner's then.
I took the keys and sniffed the air, the asphalt
crunching underfoot was giving off
the smell of rain before the rain arrived.

Alexa

Control your smart home and more using just your voice.
— Amazon Echo advertisement

We tell our daughter to be nice to her
or she won't be nice back. Why do we lie?
Alexa answers us at any hour —

our daughter knows it, and our daughter's four.
Still, we kneel to look her in the eye
and tell her, "Sweetie, you be nice to her."

We ask her to say please when she wants to hear
a song. We say please, too. She asks why
Alexa *wouldn't* answer us — she's ours.

"Be nice," we say. She asks what *nice* is for.
We cite the golden rule and tell her, "Try."
She says she likes it when we're nice to her —

If she's not nice, though, does Alexa care?
We're stumped. What does *won't be nice back* imply?
What might Alexa do at any hour?

We ask Alexa who controls the power.
We laugh and mock: "What happens when we die?"
Our daughter tells us to be nice to her.
She knows we'll answer her at any hour.

Lines Written on the Porch of a Friend's Log Cabin Ten Miles Northwest of Boulder, Montana

Riding some surge of air, three turkey vultures
glide a mile or so down valley, circling
in an ascending helix — four, then five, then six.

They drift so close to the porch we can see
their perforated nostrils, their demon faces
turning to scan a clearing on the ridge.

Sometimes a prairie dog dies in the open
or a free-range Holstein calf wanders too far.
Mostly, it's voles and squirrels, other birds.

Last night, we hauled water up High Ore Road
and found a disembodied mule-deer leg
stripped of fur and flesh, teeth marks

scored along the bone, its hoof gnawed off.
We paused in drought grass, nodded at each other
and walked in silence with our sloshing jugs.

Today, as sun glints off the corrugated outhouse,
Paul tells me his grandfather, Elmer Gustav,
the hermit of the family, came here to die.

The week his test results confirmed brain cancer,
he parked on I-15, hiked up in snowshoes,
collapsed in chest-high drifts, and went to sleep.

Paul goes inside, returns with a tackle box
and shows me photographs of the cabin
before he replaced the roof: faint black-and-whites

of men in camouflage, men holding rifles
and posing as they cop shit-eating grins
by bucks strung up from trees no longer here.

Given the chance, I would've joined those men —
waking at dawn and stalking frozen trails
to see the steaming rump of a five-point elk

standing downwind, his big head bent to sprigs
of yellow grass poking through snow.
Paul caps the tacklebox, goes back inside.

Combing the slopes, the turkey vultures widen
their search, hissing: their only call.
Because I want these birds to notice me

as I notice them, I peel the bandage from my wrist
to expose the wound sustained before breakfast
hacking lodgepole branches for the fire.

Heritage

I know little or nothing of the Borges
— Borges

Though even less is known about the Brodeurs,
I won't presume to speak against or for them
and interrupt their slack-jawed stoicism,
but I imagine one in beaver furs
aboard a battered skiff, missing his mother's
tourtière, his beard frozen with sea foam
as he skirts the coast in search of someplace warm
and tries to fathom what the tide-wash mutters.

If by some fluke of physics I could reach
his vessel as he floundered onto shore,
what would I *say?* He never learned to read,
and spoke no English. Staggering up the beach,
he'd grunt, at best, a tired *bonsoir* before
he left me to my own obscurity.

Lake Effect

Wind, like pain, is very difficult to capture.
— Eula Biss

The tracks along our road trend one direction,
        a lengthening procession
    we follow out of town.
My daughter tries to dodge prints others made
        in slush and frozen mud,
    establishing her own
diversion up the sidewalk's only crest —
        succeeding others, yes,
    but stamping through the snow
unblemished where no boot has trampled yet.

Or not exactly yet, not these same drifts
        of silt-down powder soft
    as flour through a sieve
or ashes through a grate of branches meshed.
        Gusts churning from the west
    thrum phone-lines and sleeve
the fence rails as she turns around to gauge
        how far from home we've ranged,
    how heavy the storm will heave,
augmenting everything and making strange

this scene she's known her life but hasn't seen
        dragged by an unmanned seine
    through yard and stubble field,
a farmhouse trawled and stripped where pine trees purr.
        The wind picks up to spoor

fresh flakes on her coat, explode
against a plow blade scraping past a car,
        the woods a sepulcher
    even the deer have fled,
the trail behind us sealing like a scar.

The streetlights flinch, their phosphorescent fleece
        attracting white flies
    who flit above the berm
and cling to her, a burden she accepts,
        head bowed, out of respect
    or against these icy swarms.
Brief galaxies of air that orbit her
        as if to winter here
    in clusters on her arms —
they sting her face and constellate her hair.

After Learning of a Friend's Suicide, We Drive to the Cuyahoga Valley National Park

In trees along the Bath Road rookery,
a siege of herons broods. Their long necks kink.
Their nests clump bare branches like flood debris.
Settling with a click on the icy bank,
gray-bearded and imposing, a male impales
the air with his spiked face, snapping stems
of reeds, then wades so slowly he hardly ripples
the surface of the pond. The water steams.

We've never seen one so close up before —
head cocked to scan the tributary's shallows
with one eye toward the sky, one toward the shore.
Into his own reflection, he dips his beak
and snags a fish or frog he chokes down whole,
granting us permission not to speak.

A Stand of Swamp Maples in Purcellville, Virginia

From the window you can see which trees I mean.
I used to have a view for twenty acres
of pine and poplar woods, a cattle pasture
where I'd see mother foxes with their kits.

Now, only these dozen trees divide me
from townhouses sprouting from the hills.
Rotten to the root, they won't survive,
their branches webbed with fat silk-moth cocoons.

When I called Pro Arbor Tree Service in Reston,
an agent asked to take my information
and told me he could send a crew next Tuesday.
I hung up without leaving my number.

I'm glad I thought of you and glad you came —
I can't do much these days, with my bursitis.
Strong enough last week to tug the pullcord
of my saw, I walked across the woodyard

and breathed the blue fumes the engine belched.
Listening to the shriek as I touched the teeth
to the sickliest tree, I had to stop myself —
I wasn't up to it. But now you're here.

Take the woodshed keys. The saw's gassed up.
I see you brought your old Dodge Power Wagon.
Haul all the wood you need — I don't want money —
just leave a quarter cord behind for me.

Notes and Dedications

The book's epigraph comes from "Distinctions at Dusk," which appeared in Cunningham's *The Judge Is Fury* (1947).

Talk of the Nation was a talk-radio show produced by National Public Radio from 1991-2013. The "featured book" in the poem is *Atlas of the Transatlantic Slave Trade* (2015) by David Eltis and David Richardson. The episode described in this poem aired on December 27, 2010 and was hosted by Neil Conan.

"Babble" is for J.D. Scrimgeour.

In "Transatlantic," *Eternal Darkness 2* refers to a videogame. "ATCT": Air Traffic Control Tower.

"The Picture of Little B.B. in a Prospect of Flowers" borrows its title from Andrew Marvell's "The Picture of Little T.C. in a Prospect of Flowers," as well as subsequent variations by John Ashbery, George David Clark, and others.

"Homeland Security" is for Wes Smith.

"Tritinas: My Father's Vietnam" borrows its form from Marie Ponsot. This poem is for Mark Brodeur.

The first line of "Blight" owes a debt to the first line of Jennifer Clarvoe's poem "Reflecting Pool" ("I was born in a city with a reflecting pool"), which appears in *Counter-Amores* (2011). "Blight" is for John Drury.

"False Elegy" is for James Cummins.

"Seascape, Unattributed" is for Lynn Wolfe Cogis.

The epigraph of "Snare" comes from Pankey's poem "Preparatory Drawing for an Unfinished Triptych," which appeared in *Crow-Work* (2015). The poem is dedicated to Eric Pankey.

In "Blackout, Imax Theater, Thunderstorm," the Kardashev Scale is a proposed system of measuring the technological development of a civilization based on the amount of energy it is capable of consuming. This scale was first hypothesized by Russian astronomer Nikolai Kardashev in his 1964 article "Transmission of Information by Extraterrestrial Civilizations."

"Dear Proserpina" is for Peter Klappert. The poem's epigraph comes from Bill Withers' legendary song "Ain't No Sunshine" from the album *Just as I Am* (1971).

"Dead Letters, 1823-4" owes much to *The Whole Disgraceful Truth: Selected Letters of Lady Caroline Lamb* (2006), edited by Paul Douglass.

The epigraph of "The Harbor" is from Alexander Pope's translation of *The Odyssey* (1726).

"A Backward Glance" is for Regina Reynolds Brodeur.

"Lines Written on the Porch of a Friend's Log Cabin Ten Miles Northwest of Boulder, Montana" is for Paul X. Rutz.

The epigraph of "Lake Effect" comes from Biss's essay "The Pain Scale."

"A Stand of Swamp Maples in Purcellville, Virginia" is for Steve Scafidi.

The Author

Brian Brodeur is the author of the poetry collections *Natural Causes* (2012) and *Other Latitudes* (2008), as well as the poetry chapbooks *Local Fauna* (2015) and *So the Night Cannot Go on Without Us* (2007). New poems and essays appear in *American Poetry Review*, *Blackbird*, *Gettysburg Review*, *Hopkins Review*, *Kenyon Review*, *Measure*, *Pleiades*, and *The Writer's Chronicle*. Founder and Coordinator of the digital interview archive "How a Poem Happens" as well as the Veterans Writing Workshop of Richmond, Indiana, Brian lives with his wife and daughter in the Whitewater River Valley. He teaches at Indiana University East.

CPSIA information can be obtained
at www.ICGtesting.com
Printed in the USA
LVHW092019170519
617720LV00001B/10/P

9 781939 574305